MOTIVATING SCHOOL KIDS

A book for students, teachers and parents

MOTIVATING SCHOOL KIDS

A book for students, teachers and parents

Suvasish Mukhopadhyay

Viva Books

New Delhi | Mumbai | Chennai | Kolkata | Bengaluru | Hyderabad | Kochi | Guwahati

Publisher's Note

First Published 2009, Sixth Impression 2012

VIVA BOOKS PRIVATE LIMITED

- 4737/23 Ansari Road, Daryaganj, New Delhi 110 002
  E-mail: vivadelhi@vivagroupindia.net, Tel. 42242200
- 76, Service Industries, Shirvane, Sector 1, Nerul, Navi Mumbai 400 706
  E-mail: vivamumbai@vivagroupindia.net, Tel. 27721273, 27721274
- Jamals Fazal Chambers, 26 Greams Road, Chennai 600 006
  E-mail: vivachennai@vivagroupindia.net, Tel. 28290304, 28294241
- B-103, Jindal Towers, 21/1A/3 Darga Road, Kolkata 700 017
  E-mail: vivakolkata@vivagroupindia.net, Tel. 22836381, 22816713
- 7, Sovereign Park Apartments, 56-58, K. R. Road, Basavanagudi, Bangalore 560 004
  E-mail: vivabangalore@vivagroupindia.net, Tel. 26607409, 26607410
- 101-102 Mughal Marc Apartments, 3-4-637 to 641, Narayanguda, Hyderabad 500 029
  E-mail: vivahyderabad@vivagroupindia.net, Tel. 27564481, 27564482
- Beevi Towers, First Floor, SRM Road, Kaloor, Kochi 682 018, Kerala
  E-mail: vivakochi@vivagroupindia.net, Tel: 0484-2403055, 2403056
- 232, GNB Road, Beside UCO Bank, Silpukhuri, Guwahati 781 003
  E-mail: vivaguwahati@vivagroupindia.net, Tel: 0361-2666386

www.vivagroupindia.com

ISBN: 978-81-309-1207-3

Published by Vinod Vasishtha for Viva Books Private Limited, 4737/23, Ansari Road, Daryaganj, New Delhi - 110 002.

Printed and bound by Raj Press, R-3, Inderpuri, New Delhi - 110 012.

Y0000 / M0000 / M0200

In loving memory of my mother
who never put any sort of pressure
on me during my childhood and
never compared her backbencher child
with a rank holder

Contents

Preface

I share my thoughts on motivating school kids through this book. As the name suggests, the book has various topics that motivate a school kid. This book is the outcome of my long-cherished desire to write something about motivating school kids. Though I am a faculty of engineering at postgraduate level and I have written several books for college students, my inner mind forced me to write something for the misguided school kids who are the future of the world. Millions of school kids require counselling. But few of them get it. The result is that they fail in spite of hard work.

For a long time I had a keen desire to compile important topics together in the form of a book for school students. I have tried my best to do this!

Nowadays due to cut-throat competition, comparison and humiliation done by teachers and parents, many school kids are becoming the victims of depression in their teens. Achievement is meaningless if it is coupled with stress and anxiety. In my school days I used to secure the bottom-most position whereas my elder brother was a rank holder and known for his brilliant performance and good looks. Consequently, I had to face humiliation in school and painful comparison at home. Those memories of my primary school days forced me to write this book. I can understand the problem of a school kid who is compared to his brothers, sisters and classmates. I also request the parents to go through this book. I had an open dialogue with several teachers and parents but most of the time I found them running after marks. They want children to be successful, whatever the way might be! Unless a child loves his school and subjects how can he be successful? If there is a lack in the basic concepts then there can't be any clarity in the process of learning. For this reason there is a need for a book like this which shows the perfect way to the kids towards their bright future. I have collected data from my experience and presented them in a lucid manner. I have touched all the aspects that are related to school kids. Apart from the major topics, I have taken care of minor topics also. Since my daughter is a school kid, I had the opportunity to have a keen look at the problems of a school kid for the last twelve years. I took note of her problems since 1994. She was in nursery then and in the year 2007 she appeared for SSC examination. This book is the result of my research work on school kids that has been pursued since 1994. All the problems of a school kid right from nursery to the higher grades have been analysed and presented. I had day-to-day discussion with my daughter and her friends. Their feedback about problems helped me a lot. I am completely aware of the problems and needs of school kids.

Everybody expects his or her ward to be the rank holder. But few of them know the real problem of school goers. Even a person who used to fail during his school days expects his son to be a rank holder in school. It is not possible for a poor student to have his counselling done by experts. Considering the gravity of this problem, long back I thought of this book. I address all the school kids across the globe through this book. Their difficulties created an urge within me to write this book. The difficulties of these innocent children lit different dark corners of my mind.

I expect this book will help school kids have a bright future. In a small book it is not possible to cover all the topics in a very elaborate way but the basic idea about all the topics has been given. A school kid requires knowledge of various things. An idea about all these things has been given in this book. Motivation is inspiring yourself. If there is no one to motivate you then you must motivate yourself.

In this book the ideas are explained in a simple way. No one can master a subject overnight. Even a time of ten years can be inadequate. To have command over a subject, a clear knowledge of its basics is must. It is not an easy task to motivate someone overnight. But that attempt can nullify the unwanted fear in the mind of a school kid and lift his mental state towards a higher plane.

A student requires proper guidance and once he knows the way he can move with a better progress. For a swimmer it doesn't matter whether the depth of water is ten or a thousand feet. Within every school kid there is a hidden spring of talent. I have tried my best to give an outlet to that stream.

In India school kids are misguided and they are brought up in a fear-oriented atmosphere. They have to carry heavy school bags, attend classes mechanically and rarely understand anything in the class. Gradually they become victims of failure and frustration. They are bound to be motivated and benefited after going through this book. One can enjoy this book just like a storybook.

At several places of this book I have used anecdotes, sayings and quotations from different personalities. I collected them during my academic career. The different quotations, anecdotes and sayings will reinforce the subject matter and will make it more interesting.

One must note that faith is the foundation of all relations, whether it is of a student and a teacher, father and a daughter or mother and a son. So the first step of self-motivation is to be honest to yourself.

I have tried to maintain a uniform flow of topics and present them in a simple style. I request the teachers also to go through this book for knowing the problems of their students. I do hope and trust that my readers will understand the core concept of this book and they will be able to implement it in their lives. Being a teacher, I have tried my best to make my students love their subjects. Through this book I have tried my best to inject interest for learning in the minds of school-going children.

I have visited slums and found that school kids are mostly interested in free mid-day meals rather than learning. I interviewed them. Most of them want to go to school not for education but for free 'tiffin'. We have to accept this darker and pungent side of school education in the Third World countries. If this book increases the motivation of students, teachers and the parents even by ten per cent I shall consider my effort to be fruitful.

I am deeply grateful to all the poets, writers, thinkers, philosophers and other persons whom I have referred to in this book.

Mukhopadhyay Suvasish
professor_sm@rediffmail.com

Acknowledgements

I am thankful to my daughter. I observed her throughout the complete span of her school life for the last twelve years. With each passing day I added some new things to my experience in store. I am deeply thankful to my wife Anushree who shared bad days and all the turbulent moments of my life. I thank my publisher and his team for their help. I am thankful to the readers of my previous publications.

— Mukhopadhyay Suvasish

1

School Phobia

Most schoolgoers have school phobia right from the beginning. There are various reasons for this. Generally only a few children spontaneously adapt to a school right from the beginning of their school life. The reason for this is lack of proper pre-school training. In middle-class or upper-middle-class society pre-school nursery or play group training is affordable; but the poor can't even think of it. Some reasons for school phobia are:

i) difficulty to adjust to the new atmosphere
ii) being totally detached from the parents
iii) difficulty to accept the discipline in the school
iv) tough study routine
v) fear of teachers
vi) early school timings
vii) fear of punishment
viii) dislike of homework
ix) fear of class tests
x) fear of examinations

xi) fear of class monitors
xii) fear of bullies

There are many other reasons why the small and even the older children are afraid of school and have school phobia. Nevertheless school phobia has to be tackled in a judicious way. The remedy to any kind of fear is to face it and overcome it. The best way is to jot down the main reasons that makes your mind dislike going to the school. Then analyse them one by one. In this world every problem has a solution provided the problem is understood properly. In case of any disease, if it is properly diagnosed then the treatment is easy. One needs to keep one thing in mind: that running away from a problem is not a solution. One needs to face the problem and automatically it will be solved. A child may not be able to get rid of his school phobia overnight but with persistent efforts coupled with proper counselling, the problem arising from school phobia can be solved.

2

Dislike of Some Subjects

There is no student who likes all the subjects of his curriculum equally. Even in the matter of food our choices differ. If you offer different varieties of milkshakes in a party one may prefer mango shake and someone else may prefer pineapple shake. At school one student may like mathematics the most and another's choice may be history. Generally students give less time to the subject that is of least interest to them. They give maximum time to their preferred subjects. My advice to students is: first attack the subject that you don't like. Unless you face the problem, fear will grip your mind. Accepting and facing any problem solves it to a great extent. If a rabbit closes its eyes in front of a tiger will it be spared? Obviously not! So, one must face the problem and by self-counselling one must attain a fearless state of mind.

3

Dislike of Teachers

All teachers are not liked by students. In every school there are teachers who are very popular and there is a group of teachers whom everybody hates. Students have problems with the second group of teachers. Every person has a unique attitude and the attitude of a teacher makes him or her popular or unpopular among the students. In our education system, it is assumed that the teacher is always correct, and so it is difficult for a student to give suggestions to a teacher. As every teacher has an ego, the suggestion will be considered as an undue audacity and unnecessarily the student will fall out of the teacher's favour. Why does a teacher become unpopular? There are several reasons for that. Some of the most common reasons are given below:

i) ineffective teaching
ii) wrong ideas
iii) unable to express himself
iv) can't come down to the level of the students
v) excessive ego
vi) unapproachable nature

vii) rude and vindictive nature
viii) unable to accept the generation gap

There can be many other reasons that make a teacher unhappy with his student. Once in a school, a teacher grew unhappy with the topper of the class. The teacher was unhappy because the student hadn't joined his private coaching class. That student did not like that teacher and the teacher didn't like the girl either. In another case, in one college, a group of teachers was unhappy with a student because the student belonged to a rich family and mistakenly he used to park his vehicle in the parking zone exclusively allotted for the teachers. The problems are small but people exaggerate them because of their vanity. So, one needs to think in a simple way. That will certainly solve his or her problem.

During my college days, one teacher was upset with me. I never used to attend any lectures of that professor because of his bad teaching and with each passing day his anger started increasing. In the next semester just to calm him down I attended most of his lectures (without any interest) and his anger was reduced to a great extent. Just like in medical science, in human relations also the proper prognosis and diagnosis of a problem are important. So just identify the problem, attack its root and finish it off forever.

4

Not Doing Homework

Hating homework is common among school children. I consider parents mainly responsible for this. As a small sapling requires care, watering and nurturing, a child also requires continuous monitoring. There is hardly a child who spontaneously does his homework without a reminder. The worst part of education in most of the countries is fear-oriented teaching system. Many school kids do their homework just to avoid corporeal punishment. There is no internal urge. This is like swallowing a bitter medicine.

A child is like a lump of clay. If one trains a child right from nursery, he gets properly trained. A child who was never taught discipline couldn't be made disciplined overnight at high school level.

The children need to be systematic during their school life. If a child does his homework regularly then there will be no pending work and regular workload will also be less. Most of the school kids don't do their homework on time, and if at all they do it, it is done partially and half-heartedly. Ultimately the pending work increases and regular homework gets piled up.

Some children prefer to have punishment rather than doing homework. I found a school kid saying to his parent, "What will happen if I don't do the homework? The teacher will slap me twice. I am used to it." His parents were only amused by this. This is a great mistake. Parents must not give indulgence to any wrong practice. At the same time the parents must not be too strict. Parents should be friendly with their child, and they can be the best guides. They should inculcate in the child the habit of doing things systematically so that even without any reminder they will do their homework.

Does a child have to be reminded to eat food? Generally no! He knows that he has to eat. It is spontaneous. Similarly, they should feel spontaneously that they should do their homework. Once a famous philosopher said, "Don't separate problem and solution. Mind that solution is nothing but the last part of your problem." So don't take homework as a task. Take it easy. As long as you are pre-occupied with your homework you won't feel like doing it. The moment you drop your pre-occupation, your mind will be free from all the bogus burdens and your efficiency will be manifold.

5

Fed up with the Same Lunch Pack Every Day

Children don't like to carry the same kind of food to school every day. They are often tempted by the food their classmates have brought. The nutritious food is not always the tasty. And the tasty food may have no nutrition.

When I was in school, one of my classmates was from a rich family. Every day he used to bring delicious cakes, pastries and sweets in his lunchbox, and we had simple boxed and vegetable dishes. The rich boy, however, gave his food to others and crazed for our simple dishes and bread. He was fed up with the rich food he used to get every day. He asked his parents to pack simple food for him, but they did not listen to him as they wanted to show off.

This story proves that parents should not ignore the children's tastes in the matter of food. They should be given variety.

6

Refusing to Carry Lunch to School

Some children refuse to eat. It is a common problem. The parents get panic-stricken and take the child to a doctor. But do they try to understand why the child dislikes food? The child who refuses food at home will not want to carry a lunchbox to school either.

This problem is more psychological than physical. Once a child who refused to carry lunch to school was taken to a psychiatrist. The reason she gave was peculiar: she did not like the shape of her lunchbox!

A boy used to bring home his lunchbox unopened. When he was counselled, he revealed that the container had a tight metallic lid, which he could not open. Being shy, he never asked his teacher for help. There are silly reasons behind big problems. You can get at the root of these problems only when you talk to a child in his own terms, with understanding.

7

Not Drinking Enough Water

Sometimes school children do not drink enough water. They return home with their water bottles intact. It is important to drink water frequently because 85 per cent of our body is water. Water aids metabolism and keeps our body clean by flushing out toxins. The habit of drinking water regularly should begin from childhood.

A school kid used to vomit every day after eating lunch from her lunchbox. Her lunch contained some fruit and milk products every day. She was instructed by her parents to drink water after having food. The wrong combination of fruit, milk and then water created acidity in the child's stomach and that made her vomit.

It is not healthy to drink water immediately after a meal. There should at least be a gap of half an hour. Once the parents of that girl stopped giving her the wrong food combination, vomiting stopped.

In summer one needs to drink more water. During the rainy season water must be boiled before drinking to avoid water-borne diseases like typhoid and jaundice.

8

No Interest in Extra-Curricular Activities

Extra-curricular activities are of the same importance as co-curricular activities. Generally, in a city there are few playgrounds. In villages there is plenty of space to play, which was the case also in our cities once upon a time. But due to continuous construction of buildings and growth of population we hardly find a green field in the heart of a city.

By extra-curricular activities I mean outdoor games. Today children's non-academic activities are limited to watching cartoon channels and web-browsing. Most children are glued to the TV or computer screen in their free time.

Children in the city suffer because of the very nature of city life: stiff competition, high-speed life, busy parents and small families. In India the child in the city can afford a football but has no space to play, and the child in the village has ample space but can't afford a football!

There are alternative activities for kids who don't have space to play. They can run a few rounds if their terrace is big enough. A cycle ride in the evening gives enough physical exercise and soothens the mind. So switch off the computer, and get on the cycle. Whatever extra-curricular activities children do, it must not be with some competition in mind. Sports and games must be played for their own sake if they are to be beneficial.

Some children complain that because of the pressure from studies and homework they don't find time to play. From the twenty-four hours of a day it will not be too difficult to set aside an hour for play.

You simply have to sacrifice the time you spend for TV and video games. A good habit will be formed at the cost of a bad one.

9

Facing Defeat

Victory and defeat are two sides of the same coin. As darkness makes us conscious of the power of light, defeat makes victory valuable. Defeat is not all that bad if accepted in good spirit.

We will not win every time either on the playground or in life. The bitter part of defeat is the negative comments and comparisons one has to face. The comments and criticisms are more painful than the defeat itself.

What should you do when you are defeated? Ignore people's comments. You are like a goalkeeper in a football match. If you stop the ball, people will applaud; if you miss, not only will they abuse you but also talk about all that you should have done. The irony is that the ones who advise you in defeat are those who have never won a game in their life.

We must accept the reality of defeat, and learn a lesson from defeat by analysing why we lost. It can be too costly to always learn from our own mistakes. We should also learn from other people's mistakes. To lose honestly is better than winning by crook.

10

Backbencher's Woes

In most schools backbenchers feel humiliated. 'Backbencher' is a relative term. Those who are backbenchers in a good school will sit in the front rows in an average school. Teachers, parents and seniors often create prejudices against backbenchers in other students' minds, that backbenchers are bad.

In a school students' seating arrangement is according to their height. Tall students sit at the back, those with average height in the middle and short ones in the front. This arrangement leaves no room for prejudices against anyone.

11

Forced to Lie to Parents

Some students fear their parents and lie to them without really wanting to. They do this either to please their parents or to escape scolding or punishment. For this, parents themselves are mainly responsible. If parents cannot be the friends of their children, they should at least be friendly.

12

Poor Marks in Class Tests and Assignments

Many students secure poor marks in class tests and assignments. This is due to a wrong method of answering the questions. Some of these mistakes repeat in the final examination also. If the students follow some basic guidelines, they'll be able to secure good marks in all the tests and assignments. Some important tips are given below:

i) Attend all the classes regularly and attentively.
ii) Devote at least half an hour for each subject daily.
iii) Don't have a phobia of any subject.
iv) Prepare for the difficult subjects first and then go for the easy ones.
v) Always keep a dictionary beside you.
vi) Always keep an atlas beside you.
vii) Try to present answers in a good handwriting.
viii) Write your roll number properly on the main answer sheet and on all the supplementary answer sheets.

ix) Visit the school library regularly for reference.
x) Discuss your doubts with your teachers and friends.
xi) Keep your geometry and pencil boxes tidy, and all the instruments in them must be in a ready-to-use condition.
xii) Draw margins in your answer sheet.
xiii) Adopt proper time management in the examination.
xiv) Try to avoid silly mistakes and check all the sums twice after solving them.

13

Difficulty in Getting Along

Difficulty in getting along with friends is a common problem. It is seen often in children who need to change their school frequently because their parents get transferred to new places. There are students who can mix with everyone, and there are some who are reserved and rather introvert. In school, children generally like an extrovert friend. The nature of a child depends on several parameters, mainly the atmosphere of his house and the relation that he enjoys with his parents and other family members.

Every person needs a friend to share his feelings. Right from the nursery kid to the topmost executive of a multinational company, everybody requires a friend. A friendless man is either mentally abnormal or selfish. The foundation of friendship lies in mutual faith and understanding. If you are a person who helps others, you can easily win friends and within a short period you will have many friends. On the contrary if you are of selfish and opportunist nature then most of the classmates will abandon you.

To give an example, there are two girls in a certain school of Pune. One is the topper and the other is next to her. The topper is extremely popular because while mixing with others, she never discriminates against anyone. But the second girl always reminds others by her attitude that she is superior to them. However great you may be, if you start boasting of your talent, everyone will distance themselves from you. If all your certificates are burnt, will it affect the progress of this world? Certainly not! On the contrary, if a helpful person leaves your school, then all of you will lament. We don't remember people by their degrees; we remember people by their deeds. So be helpful! It is a fact that many people in this world are bad, corrupt, dishonest, ungrateful, rude, proud and selfish. But if you also be of that type, what will be the difference between you and those people? At least you should be good and helpful. You will realize slowly and steadily that even a bad friend can be transformed. The influence of a person's mind over another person's mind is really great. You won't have any problem in getting along with your friends. A frown requires more muscles to work than are needed for a sweet smile. So why not smile and win others' hearts?

14

Language Problem

The students of vernacular medium face this problem. In most countries, English is the dominant language. In today's world, however brilliant you may be, if you are weak in English, you will be sidelined in every area. It doesn't matter whether you know your mother tongue, but you must know English very well. English is like a bridge between the external world and you.

Generally students of vernacular medium take English as a labour and somehow they pass the written examination. But whenever there is verbal communication and group discussion, they give a poor performance. Brilliant students of vernacular medium suffer just because they lack in communication skills. However brilliant you are, if you fumble and stammer you cannot clear an interview.

What is the solution for these students? Will their future be dark? Is there no way out? Well, there is a way provided you work hard. In this cyber age there are several ways to upgrade yourself. Just your wish and staunch self-motivation is required. You can improve your communication skills.

I studied in an ordinary vernacular medium school of West Bengal. Since I was in an ordinary vernacular medium school, I can understand the difficulties of these students. They suffer from an inferiority complex. I found ordinary students of reputed schools performing better than brilliant students of vernacular medium just because of their good verbal and written communication skills in English.

Practise speaking in English. If nobody cooperates with you, stand in front of a mirror and introduce yourself in English. Log on to various websites and collect learning materials for spoken English. Listen to English news and English music. You may not be able to understand even five per cent in the beginning. Don't be discouraged. Gradually you will find the taste of this language. Try to form a group of students who are just like you. Overcome shyness and start communicating in English with your friends. Form a group of six students. Five of you interview the sixth friend and in this way all of you will develop. Nothing is impossible. If a polio patient can win an Olympic medal, can't you learn English? It is not that difficult. You just require strong willpower. Once you start it, with each passing day it will be easier for you.

15

Getting Used to a New Atmosphere

Children generally do not easily adjust to a new atmosphere. This is because they are very sensitive. They do not find anyone who listens to them, and those who do load them with advices.

Here is an example of how a child learned to adapt to a new school atmosphere. Once a child's father shifted him to a boarding school against his and his mother's wishes. He was not able to adjust to the strict discipline and loneliness of the new place.

He grew morose in the evening because when he was at home every evening he would wait for his father who would bring him chocolate and pastries. He became a victim of juvenile depression, and he had to be brought back home.

When he was to go back to the boarding school after the winter vacations, his parents gave him a CD which contained pictures of all the activities the child used to do at home. Whenever he felt homesick, he was to run the CD and look at the virtual home on the screen. This helped tremendously in reducing his homesickness and he gradually adapted to the boarding school life by the end of the term.

16

Who Is a Good Friend?

In today's world a good friend is a rare thing. You may have good parents, good brothers, good sisters, good neighbours, but you should feel fortunate if you get good friends. What is a friend? A friend is one who doesn't have a blood relation with you, but who is often considered to be more important. A good friend is a person who guides you properly, who is your well-wisher and who is not jealous of you. You rarely come across such a person in today's world.

Choosing a good friend is difficult. As we grow old, the chances of finding a good and true friend reduces. Real friends can be made in school days only. At an older age what you get are colleagues, not friends.

There are two kinds of friends. The first are friends of palmy days and the second are friends of rainy days. Friends of rainy days are the actual friends. Before making a person your friend, observe him for a couple of weeks and judge him from different angles.

They are selfish who possess more but don't want to give a single grain from their stored wealth and they are selfless who share even a single apple with others. Whenever you want something from some person and you approach him, immediately you can judge his attitude. There is a group of people who bluntly refuse. Another group also refuses but that refusal is coated with a tinge of diplomacy. There is a third group also. They give spontaneously. Only the third group can be considered worth mixing with. A selfish and calculative person can't be a friend.

Once during my school days, I forgot to bring my eraser and I borrowed it from one of my classmates and after using it while returning the class teacher noticed it. There was a great misunderstanding. The class teacher thought that the other boy didn't bring an eraser and was disturbing me. The teacher got furious and punished the boy. Still the boy didn't disclose the fact. He suffered the punishment for nothing. This is an example of an ideal character.

After the class I asked him the reason why he didn't disclose the truth to save his skin. He replied, 'If I had disclosed the fact, instead of me the teacher would have beaten you. Let one be the sufferer.'

17

Good Handwriting

Handwriting of any student or any person has tremendous importance. There is an expression in English: 'love at first sight'. It is the case with the handwriting. When we see good handwriting, we instantly praise it even before judging the content. There are some things which are to be taken care of right from childhood. Handwriting is one of them. Now there will be a question. If a forty-year-old man finds that his handwriting is bad, what will he do? Will he not try to improve it? The answer is a definite yes. All the time we must remember these two words: 'I CAN'. How much we can is a different question, but certainly 'WE CAN'. There is no doubt about that. Never say 'I CAN'T'. A forty-year-old person may not be able to develop a very beautiful handwriting, but definitely with practice, he will be able to write legibly. Practice always pays. Even if improvement is slight, it is still an achievement.

18

Not Understanding Some Subjects

If you didn't attend classes regularly, you will have problems understanding particular subjects. Not all students report on the first school day of the year. Many join after a week of the start of the term. By this time the teacher would have already covered some portion of the subject. The late-joiners will find it hard to understand the subject since they didn't start from the beginning. Their understanding of the subject remains partial for the rest of the term and their interest levels low.

Once a family went to a hill station on vacation and returned a little after the school reopened. The child was worried about the school days missed. His father reassured him: 'Don't worry my boy. I'll see that your teacher allows you to attend her class. I'll get you a discharge certificate from a nursing home. It will show that you were admitted there during your absence from school.' What a bad example to set for a child! Parents are the role models for children. If they prove to be wrong models, we can't blame the children if they became bad citizens.

Another reason why certain subjects become hard is because of the gaps in background knowledge, that is, not having thorough grounding in concepts learned in lower classes. Sometimes students skip some lessons, pass the exam and get promoted to higher classes. But the advanced concepts they will now learn presuppose a knowledge of the basics.

Once a famous painter was asked whether painting was easy or difficult. He smilingly replied, 'Either it is easy or impossible!' If you love your subjects and put the required efforts then it will be easy for you, otherwise it will be very difficult. So be regular, have some proper plan in your mind and give first preference to your career.

19

Class Monitor, the Bully

The class monitor's job is to ensure discipline in the class in the absence of teachers. Usually the best student of the class is made the monitor. Often these monitors start behaving like the teacher thinking that they have great power. A good student need not necessarily be a good monitor. A monitor must have good leadership qualities and a rapport with the class.

Once in a school a boy was made the class monitor on the basis of his age. He had failed four times in the sixth class and was older than all other students. But he turned bully and began to threaten students that he would report those students to the teacher who didn't pay him a bribe of 50 paise and have them punished. How unfortunate it was that children were exposed to bribery at such a young age! Ultimately, one boy reported about this to the headmaster and the monitor was expelled from the school.

If you ever feel that the class monitor is bullying you, report it to your parents or teachers. Do not ever keep silent about these bullies.

20

Taking Part in Competitions

In every school a few students always win awards and prizes, and the rest of the students remain silent spectators. When I was in school, I was one of those who never won prizes. The reason why the majority does not win prizes is that they are demotivated through comparison to better students and criticism of what they have done.

The important thing is to participate. With self-motivation we can awaken the dormant volcano inside each of us. When you start participating in competitions, do it without expectations. Expectations cause tension and pressure. Once you do this, all that is required is practice and refinement. With time you will develop a flair and succeed in the competition.

21

Games

What game should you play for recreation and fitness? You can't play all. It is important to know which game suits you. If your neighbour's son plays cricket, should you also go for cricket? No, the game you play must suit you and your skills. If you give a football to Brian Lara and a cricket bat to Ronaldinho, can they perform like champions?

Whatever the game you play, regular practice is important. If you are not regular, success will go away. With success diversion increases and it is difficult to retain success than achieve it.

22

Sports in School

Generally in a school the students who are good in studies stay away from sports. It is a fact that the students who are good in academics are weak in sports and those who are good in sports are weak in academics. Being good at studies does not mean you need not take part in sporting activities. You should realize that all competitions in life are not for winning. When you do not win, you should cheer for those who wins.

Similarly, whenever there is a programme in the school, you should not skip it or sit at home enjoying a holiday just because you are not participating in any event. These occasions come rarely and you must not waste them away for a holiday.

In a school, a boy used to be the class monitor every year from class five onwards. When he entered class nine he was again chosen to be the monitor. But he said, 'I don't want to be the monitor for the fifth time. Let others get their chance.' This is the true sportsman spirit.

23

Principal to Watchman

Have you ever greeted your school watchman in your life? Just greet the watchman and see his reaction. We have a bad manner to address the watchman as 'watchman'. It is absolutely wrong. Everybody has a name and prefers to be addressed by that name. The watchman is older than you. So why not to address him as 'uncle'? We are always busy greeting the people in authority. How many times do they reciprocate from the core of their heart? Few times I guess! On the contrary if you greet the watchman of your school he will remember it forever.

In our residential society there was a function and all the members of the society received flower bouquets from the society and after the function each of them took it to their house. I gave my bouquet to the watchman and the glint that I saw in his eyes is still engraved in my mind. Love and help others as much as you can. If you do that your life will be full of different flavours, which are nothing but the collective blessings of the people around you.

24

When the School Starts Early

It is difficult for some students get up and go to school early in the morning. In winter and rainy season this problem becomes serious. Also, after holidays when the school reopens the students can get lazy.

When the school starts early, time management for the rest of the day is important. If a student goes to bed late because of the pressure of studies or homework, he may find it difficult to get up early. There has to be a proper plan for the day. The child must not keep his work pending for the morning. He must pack his school bag the previous night. His dress, bag, pencil box, geometry kit, everything must be kept ready. In the morning he can get fresh and leave for school after breakfast.

25

Studying in the Vacation

If you don't water a plant for a few days it starts to wither. This is what happens when students neglect their books after the annual examination. During the vacations most students don't even touch their books. During the exams they do intense study under pressure. If this kind of study routine can be maintained during vacation it can greatly help them.

Children will not easily realize the value of study during the vacation, so the parents need to advise them on the proper use of time in the vacation. Just two hours a day for study can make a great difference. This helps the students not only to learn the lessons in advance but get ahead of others the next year.

There was a student who, after her CBSE exams, bought all books of class 11 and started studying the lessons in science and mathematics. She developed an interest in mathematics and completed the class 11 mathematics syllabus before her CBSE results were out. She found the lessons easy to understand when the classes began. With the advantage of advance study she completed the lessons of class 12 while she was in class 11.

This girl then started preparing for the IIT-JEE in the time she could save. She cleared the examination and become a successful electrical engineer.

26

Scholarship Examinations

There are many scholarship examinations conducted by various organizations. A student should appear for these examinations. You may not be the winner, but these exams will train you to face competitive examinations. Many of these are objective-type tests. With repeated appearance you will acquire the skill of time management during an examination. The preparation you do for these will be useful for more tests either in school or elsewhere.

27

Quiz Competition

Quiz competition is an integral part of school and college life. If you take part in quiz competitions right from the childhood you will enhance your general knowledge to a great extent. Rome was not built in a day! No one can be a quizmaster overnight. You need to read the newspaper regularly. Many students buy books of general knowledge and start mugging up for succeeding in competitions. This way one may accumulate some stored data but acquiring general knowledge is not possible. It is a slow but steady process. Do you drink 2–3 bottles of water right at the time of breakfast? Obviously not! But if you measure the amount of water you drink in the whole day it will be approximately 2–3 bottles. It is a slow but continuous process. Same is the case with gaining general knowledge for a quiz competition. You need to go through a standard newspaper regularly and apart from that you need to read the books specially made for various quiz competitions. It will help you and the best advantage is that apart from your basic discipline you will be aware of other subjects and you will have an overall knowledge of all the subjects.

28

Laboratory Activities

A student is generally required to work in physics, chemistry and biology laboratories in a school. Students are divided into groups and given time slots to go to the laboratory and do the practicals. But the time allotted is usually not enough to gain a command over the subject. To gain proficiency one needs to repeat an experiment 3–4 times. Few students do that. If you tell your teacher that you want to do it, he will be the happiest person, and will certainly help you.

Generally in schools practicals for any subject are conducted for a single time and then at the end of the term students have to perform the practicals after a long gap. This is not of much help. One should be in constant touch with the practical part of every subject.

The internationally famous physician Dr B.C. Roy used to dissect human bodies for hours together to gain proficiency in dissection. He became one of the topmost physicians in the world. Practise as much as possible and only then will you be perfect.

29

Your School Library

Every school has a library. It depends on the school whether the library is well-stocked or not. A good library is an extensive collection of books and journals. Visiting the school library is a good habit a child should develop from his primary school days.

You must read novels, poetry and the classics, apart from books related to study, for the overall development of your mind. A library is a storehouse of knowledge and you must make full use of it. Go to the library periodically and get books issued. Return them after you finish reading, and borrow new books. General reading, in parallel to studies, is essential for your inner self to develop. Reading is the best way to enrich knowledge, and there is no substitute to reading.

Donate your old books to the school library, so that other students can benefit from you. Your individual contributions may be negligible, but if all students make this simple gesture, a school library can be enlarged considerably.

30

Your Class Teacher

In school life your class teacher plays a major role. Some teachers are strict; some are student-friendly. It is your luck what kind of teacher you have. But by virtue of discipline and hard work you must impress your class teacher. The class teacher is the representative of the headmaster or headmistress. If your class teacher is impressed with your performance, automatically the highest authority comes to know about you. Try to be regular in the class. Don't be absent from the school for silly reasons. There are many diversions in life and for them we remain absent from the school. But who is the sufferer in the long run? It is none other than you. If you miss a class, at the most you can take down the notes, but you miss the experience of being taught. If copying of the notes had been sufficient, then all the good students would have done only that. Never remain absent. Have a good relation with your class teacher. The class teacher is your moral guardian. Be respectful and do your work in a neat and disciplined way. The class teachers throughout their life remember good students.

31

What Score to Target in an Examination?

Every student must have a target score in mind while appearing for an examination. Students have subjects like English, German, Mathematics, Physics, Chemistry, History, Geography, etc. Let's assume that for each of these subjects the total marks is 100. There are many students who just want to pass the exam and they are happy with just 40 per cent marks only. It is dangerous. Never keep a low aim. If you aim for 40 you will certainly get less than that. Rarely do people reach the aim they fix. People generally attain two-thirds of their aim. If you aim for 90, you will certainly get 60 or above. So have a high aim.

Write down your target score for each subject in a sheet of paper and paste it on the wall or on a board in front of your writing desk. You will see that every time you sit at your desk you will be motivated by these targets.

32

Teachers with Different Temperaments

Sometimes it gets difficult for children to adjust with teachers of different temperaments. For this they should study the personality of teachers. It is difficult for primary and pre-primary school children. But students in higher classes are capable of judging a teacher's temperament.

It is important not to make any teacher angry. Never make a negative comment about a teacher. The teacher will most likely come to know about it and he will be permanently unhappy with you. He will henceforth assess you with a biased mind, and that can damage your career.

No teacher wants his ego to be hurt by a student. A teacher may sometimes go wrong, but you need to point it out in a polite way. Try to judge your teacher and find out what he expects from you. Some teachers adopt the right method of instruction, others encourage passive mugging up. Even when it is difficult to adjust with a teacher's attitude, you are helpless. So it is best to act according to your teacher's expectations from you.

33

School Picnic

School picnic is an occasion that children remember for the lifetime. Generally every school arranges picnic for all the classes during winter. There are a few students who never participate in the school picnic. They should.

For the junior class, the picnic spots are not far from the school. Senior classes may go on a picnic to a distant place. Winter is a pleasant time for such activities. One becomes refreshed by this kind of activities. School life is not only for academics but also for overall grooming of the student. The student gets the opportunity to visit places like hill-stations, religious places and theme parks during these picnics. So one must not stay away from the school picnic. In our busy life, a school picnic won't come frequently or according to your wish. If you don't join the picnic now, you will certainly regret it when you grow up.

34

How to Help Your Friends

The more helpful you are, the happier you are. One must help his friends and classmates. It is very easy to eat alone but one must know that he should share his food. Sharing gives a fine feeling to your inner being and unless you share you won't be able to feel it. Generally, in every school the toppers make their own group and are too proud to mingle with others. This is not at all fair. One must mingle with everybody.

Good students should teach their friends who are relatively poor in academics. There is a Japanese proverb, 'To teach is to learn twice.' I personally felt it to be true in every sphere of my life. When I was in the ninth standard there was a boy in my class who was poor financially as well as academically. I used to teach him regularly and he used to spend most of his day at my house. After my mother's death there was no one in the house except my father and me. That friend of mine used to stay in my house and all the time I used to guide him. By doing so I gained command over the subjects and the quality of learning improved. What is the use of you being strong in academics if it is of no use to others? Share your knowledge with others. They will remember you. Never be egoistic. Education, knowledge and wisdom all are different forms of bliss. They are the gifts of God. If you are blessed with those gifts don't store them, share them. Knowledge is the only thing in the world that increases by sharing.

35

Why You Should Be Helpful

One must be helpful. The whole world wants to be loved by others but there are hardly any people who want to love others. Always we expect others to help us, but how many times have we helped others? If you want to help, there are thousands of ways to do it. A simple example can be given. When you get promoted to a higher class either you sell the old books to the shops that keep old books or you store it for years together. Instead of doing this if you give them to a poor student, will it not be a kind gesture? Why not consider doing this?

Some good students are selfish, and they don't give their books or journals to others. There is valid reason behind it. A good student needs to put enormous effort for preparing a notebook or practical journal and then if he gives it to an ordinary student, he uses it carelessly and damages it.

It may be risky to share your book or journal with others but it is not risky to share your knowledge with others. Once in a school a poor student asked a doubt to the topper of his class because he had faith in the topper.

But the topper intentionally gave him a wrong answer to mislead him. This is not a healthy attitude. If you don't want to guide your friend, it's OK. But at least don't misguide him.

One should try to help others to the maximum extent for his or her pleasure. The more you help, the happier you become. It is felt in every sphere of life. You must have observed that a benevolent person is always smiling and a selfish person is always saturnine. Why is it so? This is because by helping others you can win their minds and earn their love and blessings. Others' good wishes are the fuel for your future. Always try to make those happy who seek help and who are around you.

36

Why Love Your School

It seems to be a silly, but it is an important question. One must love his school. Don't you love your house and your family members? The answer is yes. Similarly your school is nothing but an extended family. One must be attached to the teachers and schoolmates. Love has a great power. Love has the power to transform everything. Love is the force that we rarely use. With the help of love you can change the whole world. Generally, everybody wants to be loved by others but I advise you to go a step further. We usually don't mix with the children who are junior to us in the school. Just do it once and see the result.

Once in a certain school, a girl of tenth standard (she was the head girl of the school and academically she was ahead of everybody else in her class) presented a pen and a chocolate to one small kid of the third standard. She did it just out of love but the small kid was touched by it, and for her to get the pen and chocolate from the best student of the school was a big achievement. She was extremely elated and narrated the incident to her parents. The next day her parents came to meet the head girl of the school. The whole incident got great hype, and the affection of the head girl for the juniors became famous. If you love others, in return you will be showered with love and affection. You just need to have a positive mindset and helping attitude.

Every student must be attached to his school. There are students who remain in the same school right from nursery to class tenth. Some students change school after primary education. Unless one loves his school his proper mental growth will never take place. If you don't love your school, you won't like to go to school. You should be proud of your school. How many of us visit our school after we have passed out? It is a healthy habit to visit your old school at least once every year, and if possible donate some amount to the school. School is the place where you get knowledge and education. Do not forget that whatever you will be in future, it will be because of your school. School is our second home. There is hardly anyone in this world who forgets his school. All of us have some responsibilities towards our school. Let us make a plan that with the consent of the headmaster all of us will plant trees in the school compound. The sapling that you will plant today will be a big tree within a few years, and you will not be able to recognize it.

37

Gradual Change from a Lower Class to a Higher Class

As you are promoted from a lower class to the higher class, you gradually feel a change and that is obvious. A student of junior class and a student of secondary class are not supposed to face the same problems. It is a prolonged journey from nursery to tenth standard. A journey of thirteen years! In the junior class the kids have school phobia and the pressure of study is less. But one must not neglect study. The future depends on this foundation. So right from nursery classes one has to be sincere, but not serious. It is of no use to be serious because seriousness never pays.

A child must inculcate good habits right from his nursery days. If one imbibes good habits right in the childhood it becomes easy for him to be disciplined. With the increase of age it becomes difficult to mould the mindset. In different ages children face different types of problems. During the early school days, i.e. in pre-primary days, they are not taken seriously by anybody. In primary school days the kids are small and they can't express their problems. When they reach the secondary class, people start to take them seriously, but they face other types of problems. They become encumbered with huge pressure of studies and in most of the cases they don't get proper guidance. There are many children who are scared of their parents and because of this they can't even share their problems and sorrows with their parents. It is really unfortunate. Parents must be open-minded. They must listen patiently to their children.

38

Why You Should Not Avoid Geometry

Most of the school children are afraid of mathematics and especially of geometry. This is because geometry is difficult and they don't practise it. One must take care of the difficult subjects right from the beginning. On the contrary, they try to avoid it. But by avoiding it, one can't get rid of it. No one should avoid those things that are problematic. The best remedy for fear is to face the cause out of which the fear has originated. So one who finds geometry tough must practise geometry regularly at least for an hour. If you keep on doing so, your fear will gradually reduce and a day will come when you will start loving the subject. Never mug up geometry. Try to understand it. Take care of your geometry box. School kids are generally careless about their geometry box. The erasers are dirty, pencils are not sharpened and the compass is broken. It is not at all advisable. Do you wish to have a shabby look during any occasion? Certainly no! When you want to be neat and tidy, why not keep your geometry box the same way?

From the geometry box of a school kid it is known how sincere he is. So be sincere and practise. Regular practice doesn't have any substitute.

39

Your School Uniform

I have seen students of rich parents in shabby school uniforms. Their parents are to blame for this. The shape of your school uniform reflects your attitude towards studies.

Generally students use one set of uniform for many years, letting it fade and look dirty. It is better to change the uniform every academic year. Also, don't wear the same set of uniform on consecutive days. Your school uniform should be clean, free of odour, and properly ironed. There is a saying in English: 'Apparel makes a man.'

Your uniform does not need to be expensive, but it should be clean and decent. Remember that hundreds of people see you every day and judge your appearance. A boy used to be always neatly dressed. One day, for some reason he had to wear his uniform without ironing it. One of his friends was quick to comment: 'Didn't you iron your dress today?' This incident proves that people always notice mistakes, even though they may pay no attention when you do the right thing. So have an appearance that would please the world.

40

School Canteen

Most schools have a canteen. But eating at the canteen frequently is not a good practice for school children. Today's fast food culture is pushing us towards an unhealthy lifestyle. Instead of home-cooked food and fruits, we eat fast food like cakes, pastries, burgers, pizzas, etc. This is the reason why you should avoid eating at the school canteen. Whenever you have to, avoid unhealthy items and soft drinks and go for natural things like coconut water. It is very important to develop good food habits from a young age.

41

Study Trip

The study of some subjects, like History, is not complete without a study trip to a place of some importance. All of us have read about the Ajanta and the Ellora; but how many have visited them? Study trips make education live.

It is not practical to take students to every place of historical importance. However, taking them to places nearby will not be difficult. Students in a school in Agra can go to the Taj Mahal, those in Maharashtra can visit the Ajanta and the Ellora caves, and students in Delhi can go to the India Gate and Qutub Minar.

Sometimes schools take their students to large factories or laboratories to show them how Physics and Chemistry are used in the industry. Besides, they also need to visit subject-specific exhibitions to have a wider understanding of what they study from books.

A visual impression never gets erased from the mind, while what you have read is quickly forgotten. So students should not miss any study trip that the school organizes.

42

Your Style of Presentation

You may be an intelligent student, but during an interview or seminar the interviewers keenly observe your skill of presentation. There are many intelligent students who are scared of public speaking and they have inhibitions about facing an audience. They excel in written examinations, but during any interview they become nervous at the sight of the examiners or interviewers.

So, one needs to come out of this veil of fear. To shake off shyness and inhibitions, right from the childhood one must participate in small functions. If you are confident to face an audience then 90 per cent of the problems related to the presentation are solved. Nowadays all presentations are made in PowerPoint. You must learn to prepare slides and while preparing the slides you need to take care so that maximum amount of information is presented by using minimum numbers of slides. The slides should not be clumsy. Sometimes instead of writing elaborately, the presentation can be done with the help of a bar chart or graph. Pictorial presentation carries more meaning. Good presentation is an art and you need to master it.

43

Saturday – Half-day or Holiday?

Some schools have a five-day week. For them Saturday and Sunday are holidays. For some schools Saturday is a half-day. Most students do not know how to use the Saturdays when they have a full or half holiday. Most of the students waste this day. The students of the schools that have Saturday a holiday generally get up very late on Saturdays, and due to late start of the day everything is procrastinated and postponed.

If you really want to extract the essence of a day, then start it early. If you get up at 9 in the morning and start your day at 11, then by the time you will be active the sun will be in the western sky. So if it is a holiday, plan it properly. If you don't want to read, it doesn't matter. But leave your bed. Watch TV or listen to music. But leave your lethargic attitude. If you become lethargic right from school days, what will happen in the future?

Do whatever you like, but be active. If Saturday is a half-day, come back home after school and after changing your uniform have some food and then go out to play.

The real pleasure of Sunday lies in Saturday evening. Try to complete all the pending work of the week by Friday evening and enjoy Saturday to the fullest.

44

Television and Its Impact

Most parents think that television is a bane for the children and television hampers studies. But they are wrong. By disconnecting the cable parents may feel that they did a great job. But actually it doesn't help. You can physically control a person but not his mind. If you cut the cable connection you stop your child from watching TV, but the urge to see the favourite programmes does not go away. What you need to do instead is to train the child to make maximum use of the time he spends to watch TV. In our cities children don't have enough space and field to play. They are satisfied with their cartoon channels. The parents should not snatch even this minimal pleasure from them.

45

Essential Qualities of a Student

Here is a list of qualities that every student must strive to cultivate:

i) hardworking nature
ii) punctuality
iii) imagination
iv) power of expression
v) attentive nature
vi) reading habit
vii) flaming enthusiasm
viii) noble ambition
ix) politeness
x) sincerity
xi) self-discipline
xii) curiosity
xiii) creativity
xiv) regularity

Apart from these there are many other qualities that one should have. However, if a student has these fourteen qualities, it will be more than enough to succeed in examinations and in life.

46

Obedience Pays

Obedience is the capital of student life. A teacher can accept a less intelligent or even a dull student, but it is really difficult to tolerate the arrogance and aggressiveness of an intelligent student. The world is sad, bad and mad but it expects you to be good, humane and jolly. This is the crux of life. Even a sadist teacher expects his students to be polite. The fact is that a corrupt person likes an honest person and an angry person expects you to be polite.

For every student obedience is very important. Sometimes a brilliant student has a better understanding of the subject than the teacher, and this student stops to show any respect to the teacher. Even when the student does not express his disrespect verbally, the teacher can read it from his body language. After all, the teacher is much older than the students, and he deserves that respect. By being angry, aggressive and boastful you harm yourself. Try to be polite and obedient. The true essence of education does not lie in your degrees. It lies in your behaviour.

47

How to Increase the Level of Knowledge

There is no substitute for systematic study. One must have regular practice. It is easy to read a book in one day, but if you need to read ten pages per day it becomes difficult to maintain the regularity. So first strive to became regular.

When I was in sixth standard, I secured only 42 marks out of 100 in Mathematics. It was a black spot in my mark sheet and all my family members were unhappy with me except my mother. Then she suggested that I solve 25 sums every day. The advice was simple and effective. Before going to the bed every night I needed to check whether I had solved 25 sums. There were days when I didn't get time or intentionally avoided doing the exercise. But at the end of the day when I found that the required number of sums was not solved then I had to solve them before going to bed. In this way I made it a regular practice. After two years in eighth standard I secured 96 marks out of 100 in Mathematics. The saddest thing is that my mother passed away before the publication of the result. The gardener who planted the sapling was not alive to see the flowers.

48

What Should You Do If Anybody Teases You?

It is a common phenomenon in every school that a group of students tease another group of students. Given below is a list of common reasons why some children tease others:

i) if a student is short
ii) if the student has a stammering problem
iii) if the student is very fat or very thin
iv) if the student has some speech-related problem
v) if the student is taciturn
vi) if a student has problems in his family

These are some of the causes for which a student may be the victim of teasing by his classmates or by a group of seniors.

Note one thing. Whenever you are being teased, try to find out the reason behind the teasing. If possible try to get rid of that in due course of time. Once in a school there was a girl in the eighth standard. She was unusually fat. For that the students of her class and senior class used to tease her and used to call her 'moti,' which means 'fat girl'.

Initially she used to get angry and gradually teasing became a routine affair. Then she got serious. She started running two kilometres every day. Within a year she reduced her weight by eleven kilograms.

Never tolerate teasing. If possible try to get rid of the cause for which you are being teased, and if not possible, bring it to the notice of your teachers and parents. If you silently suffer teasing, it can have psychological effects. Why should you suffer for no fault of yours?

49

Corporal Punishment

Corporal punishment is now outdated. By beating a child you can't bring him to the right track. There is an old adage, 'Silence is prudence.' One line of correct counselling is more powerful than ten slaps. Initially students are scared of physical punishment. But if they regularly face physical punishment and assault, they get used to it and no longer fear it. They know at most they will be beaten, nothing more than that. So physical punishment is not a solution at all. You can bring the students to the right track only by counselling. Love is the greatest force in the world. It has the potential to transform a human being. Never allow yourself to be the victim of physical punishment. If you ever face physical punishment, immediately bring it to the notice of your principal and parents.

50

The Importance of Your Feedback

The concept of feedback was not known in our country a decade and a half ago. Everybody requires feedback after performing, whether he is a cook, a teacher, a singer or a doctor. People's feedback will help you to detect your faults and help you to improve.

Your feedback is important for your teachers. A teacher should have some of these qualities:

i) ability to present the subject matter properly
ii) clarity in his voice
iii) ability to communicate properly
iv) punctuality
v) down-to-earth attitude and approachability
vi) caring nature
vii) proper knowledge of the subject
viii) ability to complete the syllabus on time
ix) ability to guide properly for the examination
x) thorough practical knowledge

There are teachers who have huge knowledge but fail to communicate effectively. Some other teachers have limited knowledge but can present that knowledge in a simple and effective way. So students are the best judges of teachers. If the students give their feedback, the teachers will come to know about their strong and weak points. Based on this feedback the teachers can improve their teaching.

51

Your School Shoes, Watch, Umbrella, Raincoat, etc.

Every day you wear school shoes and your wristwatch. When it rains, you carry an umbrella or wear a raincoat. You need to learn how to maintain your school accessories. Your school bag should be cleaned regularly and your watch should be in running condition. Your watch can be fast by 5–10 minutes but it should never run slow. Your umbrella or raincoat should be in proper condition. The umbrellas are often broken and raincoats dirty. The students don't clean the mud spread on the raincoat.

In brief, the students should not be indifferent to their school accessories. They should themselves polish the shoes regularly. If any student does his own work right from his school days, he will be self-reliant and independent. It will make him bold and smart. Even if you belong to a rich family, try to do your personal work on your own.

52

Is Mobile Phone Required?

Should school students carry mobile phones? Students in cities do need mobile phones. But they should not be given mobiles before eighth class. For most students mobile phone is just a toy and use it to exchange fun stuff through SMS. Deprived of quality playgrounds and outdoor activities, children in our cities use their mobile phones as pastime devices

Students will need some advice on how and when to use mobile phones. Never use the phone while walking in the street or crossing the road. Don't attend calls while cycling. One moment of carelessness can cause an accident that will permanently change your life.

Once a student was coming back from his tuition classes at 9.30 in the night. There was a heavy rain and his cycle tyre got punctured. There was no telephone booth nearby. Luckily, he was carrying a mobile phone, and he called his brother, who came and took him home. Mobile phone can be useful in an emergency.

53

Your School Garden

Every school has a garden. But students rarely care for the garden. This is not a healthy habit. All of you must take some initiative to make the school garden more beautiful. Once a boy from Pune went to Uttarakhand (a northern state of India). In Uttarakhand he came across a special variety of flower and he liked it very much. That boy was fond of gardening. While returning he brought a sapling and donated it to the gardener of his school. The gardener planted it and took adequate care. By his care and nurture he was successful in growing the sapling. After few years the boy passed his secondary examination and left the school, but he left behind a permanent mark of his affection for his school. From one sapling there grew many and today the school is famous for that unique species of flower, which is available only in Uttarakhand. Take an interest in your school garden and do whatever you can to beautify it.

54

Your Playground

You may have a playground either in your school or near the place you live. Good playground for children are rare in our residential localities. Nowadays school is the only place where you find a playground. If you don't have a playground, you can manage with a park.

You should go to the playground or park every day and walk barefoot on the grass for at least fifteen minutes. In city life we are never in touch with nature. One should have a feel of the ground every day. With the advancement of technology we are moving farther away from nature. We forget the soft sea breeze and welcome the air-conditioned confinement of multiplexes.

You can revive the lost contact with nature. Touch the grass and touch the glossy leaf of a tree. Have the feel of the dewdrops that are waiting for you in the early morning over the grass in your playground.

55

Your School Bag

As you go from a lower class to a higher class the numbers of your subjects increase and you will begin to use more textbooks and notebooks. Correspondingly, the size of your school bag gets bigger with each passing year. There are many students who just throw the bag after returning from school. This throwing is nothing but the manifestation of anger with some subject teacher or with anyone else. If you throw a heavy bag full of books and notebooks, the bag gets damaged especially at the corners. Few parents buy the children a second school bag within the same academic year. They say, 'It's you who damaged it. Get it repaired and continue. Next year we will think of buying a new bag.'

Many of us are indifferent to things of use. If you need a thing regularly then why not take care of it? I know the answer. When you don't like something, you become indifferent to it. Parents must try to cultivate in children a love for their books and studies in general from an early age.

56

The Pencil Box

Once in a school I conducted a survey. I checked the pencil boxes of a hundred students. Those students were chosen at random from various classes starting from sixth class to class ten. I didn't find a single pencil box which contained pencil in proper condition. Most of the pencils were broken and not sharpened. Many students had chewed one end of the pencil. The children are careless, and parents and teachers do not bother.

It is the parents who should teach children about these. If the teachers begin to take care of each student's pencil box and school bag, they will not get time to teach.

In our colony there was a lady. Her son used to prepare for his exams till midnight and she used to sit by his side. Once I asked her, 'Why don't you sleep?' She replied, 'I am just his inspiration. If I sleep, he will feel demotivated. Just to inspire him I sit by his side without disturbing him.' This is the perfect approach. She was practically illiterate, but she understood the basic philosophy of the mother-child relationship. If every parent becomes this sincere, the life of all the students will change.

57

Your Music Class

Music is not taught in all schools. There are many school kids who have a liking for various kinds of music and musical instruments. It may be Indian classical music, western music or instrumental music. It is not possible to go to the music class every day. Generally it is once or twice in a week. There are many students who start practising music or some instruments right from a tender age. But most of them leave this good habit when they reach higher classes. You should never stay away from such good habits. There are many people who left their good careers in music for academic purposes. Ultimately they lost out on both. They left their music career, and neither could they do anything worth mentioning in their academic career.

So pursue good habits like music. It will certainly reward you. Unless you pursue it at a professional level, it won't give any monetary return. But it will certainly soothe your inner being. Music gives peace to your soul. So never leave your music class and be sincere to it.

58

Your Bookshelf

When I visited many homes with school-going children, I found that the children's bookshelves were generally untidy. Books were not kept in proper order but thrown around. If you ask for a particular book, the children fluster and are not able to locate it in their own bookshelf.

Arranging books properly means ordering them subject-wise or according to size. A well-kept bookshelf makes finding books easy. Keeping books haphazardly reflects your indifference towards your own career. To an extent the parents are responsible for the mess. They instruct their children to put away the books after study, and the children do it casually. Moreover, children damage their books by dumping them thus. When they pull out a book from the bottom of a pile, it collapses bringing every book down.

All children need to show a little care for their books and love for their subjects of study.

59

Parents' Expectations

Children get stressed when the parents' expectations of them are too high. Many parents who criticize children for not performing up to their expectations forget how badly they had performed when they were children. Comparison with other children or siblings can worsen this. There is nothing more insulting than negative comparison.

Once a woman took her two sons to a famous school for admission. After the screening test only the older one was selected for admission. Instead of admitting the successful older son to that school, the woman took the children home and, a few days later, admitted both in a less famous school. She said: 'If I had admitted the older one to the prestigious school and the younger one to a lesser school, the elder boy would develop a superiority complex and the younger one would be its victim.'

Don't compare anyone or be the victim of negative comparison. If your parents compare you with your brother or sister let them know of your protest.

60

Discovering the Most Important Person in Your School

How do you discover the most important person in your school life? He may be a teacher, your class teacher, a laboratory assistant or even a peon. The person who inspires and motivates you the most is the most important person in your school life.

There was a brilliant girl in a Pune school, and everybody liked her for her academic achievements and down-to-earth nature. All the teachers supported her, but a storekeeper of the school inspired her the most. That gentleman always used to motivate her. Once she wanted some graph paper from the store. It was out of stock. The storekeeper went to a nearby shop and bought a few sheets of graph paper for that girl and when she wanted to pay him the amount he refused to take it. That gentleman was a key motivator in the life of that brilliant girl.

In later days she became very successful. After completing her studies she took up Finance Management and presently she is the CEO of a big company in San

Francisco. She recently visited Pune and her school. First she met the storekeeper. Then she met her teachers.

61

Importance of Marks

A student who misses a golden chance just for one mark knows the value of marks. I have already discussed the role of marks and given tips on how to score more. It would seem that the whole book is written about how to study and score more. The famous book of Nirad C. Chaudhuri, *The Autobiography of an Unknown Indian*, is an autobiography and at the same time it is the narration of the ancient and contemporary history. This book will be remembered more for its historical importance. Similarly, this book definitely gives a clear idea about scoring more in an examination, but at the same time it embraces all the aspects of a student's life. I do hope this book will help you to score more in every aspect of your life. All the difficulties which the students come across are discussed in detail. If others can score more, why not you? You too can score more. There have been many promising lives that became mundane because of a low score. Don't be a wilting leaf. Be a leaf which is green and glossy. Only your willpower can make you prominent.

62

How to Develop Interest in History

There is a group of students who have tremendous allergy to the subject of History. Whether a subject is easy or hard, interesting or boring, depends on the subject teacher. A good teacher is able to create your interest even in a subject that is considered boring. On the contrary, if the teacher is bad you may lose your interest in subjects like Science and Mathematics. History is a subject in which generally students go for sheer mugging up. That is absolutely wrong. There are better ways to study History. Try to see the pictures of different places and visit places of historical importance. Don't take the subject of History as a task, take the textbook as a storybook and in your leisure slowly go through the whole textbook and then start reading again from page one. Then try to answer the questions that are given at the end of every chapter. If you sincerely stick to it then gradually interest will develop. A student who loves one subject may not like another to the same extent. But don't neglect any subject. If you neglect any subject, you will develop a phobia and your performance will be affected.

63

Language Problem and Solution to It

'The only thing that stands between a man and what he wants from life is often merely the lack of will to try and lack of faith to believe that it is possible.'

— Richard M. Devos

There are students from vernacular medium who face a great difficulty in their professional education where English is used as the medium of teaching. I have witnessed many incidents where students failed to express their feelings because they didn't have the capacity to express their feelings. It really becomes very painful when you are unable to express your inner feelings just for the lack of fluency in English.

I remember one specific incident. On one winter afternoon I was busy reading a technical paper. Suddenly I saw one of my favourite students standing outside my cabin. His name was Salim. He was a very talented boy. He was from the Solapur district of Maharashtra. He was very sound in mathematics, but it was impossible for him to communicate in English. That made him develop an inferiority complex. For this problem there is no panacea or instant solution. Only consistent practice can produce some results. I suggested that he speak in English with his roommates. His roommates were good enough to cooperate with him. Next day Salim came along with his roommates. I told those two boys to help Salim. I advised him to get rid of stammering while communicating in English. It didn't matter if it was wrong, but speed and overcoming shyness were very important. After one month Salim met me again.

Late afternoon light flashed on his innocent face. He looked partially confident. He started communicating in English. It soothed my soul.

64

Knowledge of English

Knowledge of English may not be something to be proud of, but if you don't know it you are in for a disadvantage. This is a serious problem for students whose medium of education is not English but another language. It is no surprise that even many postgraduates of our country fail to communicate well in English. This is often because of shyness and fear of making mistakes. Learning anything at a later age proves difficult, like swimming and cycling for example. In our country there are two groups of students: one educated through the medium of English, and the second, taught through an Indian language. The second group is often poor in English. While communicating with students of English medium, they suffer from an inferiority complex. They cannot express even things they know well. There are many who cannot write a simple letter in English. They generally tend to avoid the use of English. They try to manage all the odd situations with a passable knowledge. They show their hatred for the English language. The hatred for English is nothing more than a disguise for their feeling of inferiority. In the era of privatization, when there are few government jobs waiting for us, a working knowledge of English is essential.

65

Crafts Class

Generally crafts class is a part of the primary curriculum. All the students may not have interest in the crafts class. The students who have a bent for fine arts may be interested in the crafts class. Several times the parents help the children with their craft work and the children submit the models to the school that are actually made by the parents. It is an open secret; still everybody keeps mum. In India unless a subject becomes a part of the syllabus of the secondary exam we don't take it seriously.

In the craft class the teachers give training in making paper models, paper flowers and several other things. So the child must have a knack for drawing and fine arts. The parents have a great role in this. The parents who have interest in fine arts and drawing motivate their children for the craft class.

66

Preparing for the Examinations

Generally students don't study regularly throughout the year. They don't even read their notebooks completely. Many times for vague reasons they remain absent from the school and afterwards copy from someone else's notes. Sometimes they simply xerox it and attach it to their notebook. Bunking classes frequently makes them lose interest and it becomes difficult for them to catch the thread. Due to all these reasons they permanently lose interest and start scoring less in the exams.

Many parents are obsessed with their children and they think that their wards are extraordinary. There is no substitute for regular studies and practice. Success can't come overnight. The tree that gives sweet fruits must have been nurtured and cared for for a long time. Behind a good result there must be a prolonged effort. A good result in any exam is not magic. It requires strong determination, dedication, good planning and consistent hard work.

67

Your Study Table

Your study table speaks of your sincerity. Your study table must be clean and decent. It must contain the following things:

i) all the required books
ii) the required guides
iii) a personal computer or a laptop
iv) dictionaries
v) a globe
vi) punching machine
vii) paper
viii) stapler and staples
ix) pins and pin cushion
x) paper weights
xi) all the instruments required for geometry
xii) set of sketch pens
xiii) refills of different colour inks
xiv) plastic tape
xv) study schedule placed below the glass
xvi) all the reference books

68

Your Timepiece

To get up at a regular time, you need to set alarm in a timepiece. You must take due care so that it doesn't run slow and you need to ensure the cell isn't dead.

Once a student set alarm in his timepiece for the day he had the exam of mathematics. The exam was to start at 9 a.m. He studied up to 3 a.m. and then set alarm for 6 a.m. But when he got up he found it was 9 a.m. He was shocked. When he looked at the timepiece, he found that it had stopped at 4.56 a.m. The cell was very old. One may say that the watch betrayed him. But I would say that machines never betray. If we, who maintain the machines don't take care of them, they will stop functioning. The boy had a lesson for lifetime. He rushed to the exam hall and reached an hour late. He was not allowed in. From this incident you should understand the importance of your timepiece.

69

Your Water Bottle

The title of this chapter may make you laugh. But in school life right from the nursery to junior college you require a water bottle. Only the shape, size and design of the bottle changes from class to class. A kid of Junior KG carries a very colourful but small bottle. The students of a senior class may carry water in a simple plastic bottle. As children grow older they stop to care about colour and design. All they want is a handy bottle that can carry enough water for them.

Only one thing is important. Sometimes a child does not finish all the water he carried to school in the bottle, and brings the bottle back with some water left in it. He does not take out the bottle from the bag, and the next day fills fresh water over the stored water, making all water stale. The water remaining in the bottle should be thrown out and the bottle washed every morning. A thorough cleaning of the bottle is essential once in a week.

70

Importance of Communication

Proper and fast communication is essential in today's life. If you don't know how to communicate, then you are an odd man out in this age of fast communication. There are several mediums of communication and the most modern and the most efficient method is the Internet. Email is the most powerful medium of communication. Just imagine, one single click of a mouse in the corner of your room sending your message to someone who is thousands of miles away from you.

Good teachers are also good communicators, and a true master does communion. A master is one step ahead of a teacher. Timely communication can save a lot of time. There are several methods of communication. Often we give the address of one friend to another, but along with the address if we give his phone number and email ID, it makes the communication easy. I have seen many people who don't have their email IDs. Some students do have mail IDs but don't use them. If you want to enjoy communication, you have to use the Internet as much as possible. Proper communication is a skill and an art too.

71

Courtesy Pays

However intelligent a student may be he must be courteous. If a student is less intelligent, it doesn't matter but he must have courtesy and manners. We are often taught to respect our seniors. But you need to respect your juniors also. For our juniors we can show our respect in the form of love.

In a famous school one boy used to get the first rank every time. Once he stood second, and after checking the papers the principal of the school discovered that the teacher of Mathematics had made a mistake in totalling the boy's marks, and because of her mistake the boy stood second. After the correction the boy got his first rank. The boy's parents came and insulted the Mathematics teacher for this. Their ego was hurt. The Mathematics teacher felt very sorry. What she did was not intentional. When the parents insulted the teacher the boy was not present. When he came to know of the incident, he went to the teacher and apologized for the misdeed of his parents. This is an example of courtesy. If you are correct in manners and etiquette, everybody will like you. Your friends and teachers will remember your marks and success for a couple of months, what they will remember forever is nothing but your good nature.

72

Elective Subjects

At school level there are few elective subjects. But at the junior college level you have to choose an elective subject. While doing that keep in mind these:

i) You should be at ease with the subject you choose.
ii) It should be a subject that will help you in the long run.

Sometimes false pride makes students choose subjects that don't suit them. For some time they pride themselves in their chosen subject, until they start paying the price for the mistake.

In a school in Maharashtra three languages were compulsory: English, Hindi and Marathi. There were two options for the fourth language: Sanskrit and German.

A girl who was average in studies wanted to opt for Sanskrit. But her status-conscious father forced her to take up German. The girl, who didn't even have good English, fared miserably in German.

What do we learn from this? We must ask ourselves what suits us – what we are good at. This will stop us from taking wrong decisions knowingly. Listening to ourselves determines our success to a great extent.

73

Fixing Your Goal

Students must not be overambitious. They must not be crazy for success. Students and parents are in a rat race for professional degrees, which they want by hook or crook. J. Krishnamurti has said: 'What you call happiness is the outcome of getting what you want.' In this world people are always unhappy. The moment one wish is fulfilled, they start chasing the next. At the end they feel dissatisfied with all they have got. There is a major difference between ambition and craving. If one chases something without realizing his limitations, failure will be the result. We have to be realistic and logical in this respect. If we can maintain a judicious balance between our mental world and the material world, we can be considerably free from irrational cravings. Craving for more money and lack of good education lead us to think irrationally. David Frost has said, 'Don't aim for success. If you want it, just do what you love and believe in, and it will come naturally.'

If we try hard instead of dreaming, we realize that the possibilities have no end.

74

Learn from Mistakes

Everyone must learn from one's own or others' mistakes. It is costly to learn from one's own mistakes. Learning from a mistake means not repeating the same mistake Behind every mistake there is a cause, and learning means discovering the actual cause behind the mistake. He is an intelligent man who learns from his own mistake, but the person who learns from others' mistake is a wise man. The span of life is too small, and within this small span if every time we keep on learning from our own mistakes, then it will be at the cost of our life.

We must remember one thing. Failure is not the ultimate end, but only a delay. Whenever any failure occurs due to any mistake, we become the victims of frustration. If the same mistake is repeated, the result is repetition of the failure. So when there is a failure, we should accept it and admit it too. We must not be depressed. We must learn from the failure and we must be careful so that it doesn't repeat in future. We must not blame others. Generally when we face any failure, we shift the responsibility to others and when we get success, we want to take the complete credit.

This fact is observed since the dawn of human civilization. This is an ingrained quality of human character.

Here I want to share an interesting incident. In the year 1999 one of my students failed in the GATE examination due to lack of time management. He met me and I counselled him for hours together. He could realize his weak points. He was a good student, but he didn't know time management. In 2000 again he appeared for the GATE examination, and he was one of the top rankers of the country. What a dramatic change! The change took place because he had learned from his mistakes. In 1999 also he would have passed by securing a marginal score, but in 2000, because he received proper counselling and introspection, the candidate was one of the top rankers of GATE in India.

75

How to Develop Your Personality

> 'There are millions of ways to have a personality, but there is only one way to have individuality.'
>
> — Osho

Personality is a very important parameter in a person's life. An educated person without personality is bound to fail in his personal as well as professional life. Individuality is nothing but personality focused in a direction. There are certain factors which control your personality. Some of them are given below:

i) the way you talk
ii) the way you walk
iii) the way you dress
iv) the way you eat
v) the way you share your feelings and emotion
vi) the way you react to silly things or silly jokes
vii) the way you react to guests, strangers and visitors
viii) the way you react to failure

ix) the way you react to some financial gain or benefit
x) the balance of your temper

There are many other points, but these are some of the very important points which determine the personality of an individual. A man with a good personality is never afraid of silly things and has a fighting spirit in the time of difficulty. A man with a good personality is not afraid of anybody. The mission of a man with conviction is: 'Never surrender, make yourself do it.'

With a good personality it becomes easy to survive in this world and the possibility of getting noticed among others is much higher. A qualified man without any personality can only be compared to a joker. People with a strong personality never compromise. They never do those things for which the mind doesn't give a signal. You must have a good personality, but good personality must be accompanied by creative and positive thoughts. Good personality and positive thoughts are complementary. They together create great things. A man with good personality never gives in to a negative mentality. Negative mentality is more corrosive than negative results, because a negative result is nothing but the by-product of a negative mind.

76

Managing Time

'Yesterday is a cancelled cheque, tomorrow is a promissory note, and today is the ready cash. Use it.'

— Anonymous

He is intelligent who knows how to use time. Worthy use of time is an art. Everybody gets twenty-four hours per day. How he spends it differs from person to person. Right from my childhood I have often heard a common saying, 'Don't waste time.' Do you think you can waste time? How can you waste time? You can waste something that belongs to you. You can waste money if you have it. But no one possesses time, so time can't be wasted; it can only be used. Using your time in an optimized way is time management. For the proper growth of a successful career, time management is essential.

I was once on a train from Pune to Kolkata, which travels 2020 kilometres. I was reading a book during the journey. The other passengers, who seemed to be enjoying themselves at the start of the journey appeared bored the next morning. Thanks to my book, I didn't have a single moment of boredom. A book helps and you make good use of the free time available to you.

You must learn the art of managing your time at your age. If you didn't know time management when you are in school, you wouldn't know it when you are in college.

77

The Golden Rules for Every School Kid

In the beginning most of the things seem to be easy but when we try to do them, we face many obstacles. There is no substitute for discipline. If a student is disciplined, success is bound to be his. It takes a lot of time to create something but destruction takes only a couple of moments. It takes many years to construct a beautiful tower but an earthquake can ruin it within a couple of seconds. So for every student it takes staunch efforts and a long time to accomplish success. It is easy to achieve success, but it is difficult to maintain it.

Here are my 'ten golden rules' for success that any student can follow:

i) A student must go to school every day. Without a valid reason he must not remain absent from school. Due to some unavoidable reason if he misses a class, then he must collect the notes and study them before attending the next class.
ii) Every day, devote half an hour to each subject.

iii) A student must have his own textbooks, drawing instruments and other necessary things.

iv) A student must have a study routine.

v) He must understand the basics of every subject. For the subjects of science, the knowledge of basic mathematics is essential. Refer to the old textbooks of the earlier classes when required.

vi) The students should form teams, so that they can exchange views and thoughts through group discussions. It will help them in gaining fluency in English.

vii) A student must think positive and be optimistic. One must not be pessimistic. Don't form any opinion about a subject before getting to know it better.

viii) Solve the question papers of the last 3–4 examinations for each subject. It is an examination-oriented method of study.

ix) Don't skip any chapter. Don't treat any portion of the syllabus as optional. The whole syllabus must be completed. Don't differentiate between easy and hard subjects. The quality of the food is important, not the quantity. All the subjects must be studied with equal sincerity.

x) Never allow your seniors and classmates to influence you in the wrong way.

Have a higher aim, and you will achieve it by dint of hard efforts coupled with intelligent planning. Have a fellow feeling. Don't have a selfish attitude. Help your friends, and do a good teamwork. If any student follows these ten golden rules, he is bound to succeed.

78

Accept Unexpected Results and Failures

Our life is very long. It is not the journey of a few days or a few months. Each individual has to experience the taste of failure in his life. Only the number of failures or degree of failure varies from person to person. There are many reasons for failure. Always you may not be responsible for your failure. Sometimes they come unexpectedly. In most of the cases failure is confused with academic failures, but there are many other types of failures. Sometimes we get bad results unexpectedly. As an example I would like to share one incident. One of my students named Thomas John had a very good GRE score and the score of his TOEFL was also good. He applied to ten universities of the USA. He was good-looking, smart, well-mannered and had a good family background. I had recommended him strongly, and he had two more good recommendations from two other faculties. His academic progress was consistently good. In spite of all these John failed in the visa interview. He appeared for the second time and failed again. After this he was disheartened and lost all the enthusiasm and zeal to pursue higher studies in the USA. After one year again he appeared for the visa interview and failed again. The reason of his failure is still mysterious. He had to accept his failures. Failure is painful, but we can't run away from it. It is advisable to turn that failure into the cause of a success. Never stop after any failure. There is a saying,

> 'Failure is the only opportunity to begin again more intelligently.'
>
> — Henry Ford

The state of one's mind after failure can be compared to the silence of the huddle of trees before a storm. One must have the willpower to turn the tearful eyes into eyes aglow with success.

79

Importance of Discipline

Importance of discipline is appreciated by the disciplined people and felt by the indisciplined. Often we confuse between these two words 'discipline' and 'practice'. Truly speaking, good practice leads to a disciplined lifestyle. Only practice is not enough; emphasis must be given on correct practice. The word 'discipline' comes from 'disciple'. For understanding life you have to understand yourself. A disciplined man knows the values of little things in life. Success is nothing but the integration of small things done in a disciplined manner. Behind every success there is discipline. When we see an athlete winning the gold medal in the Olympics, we applaud him for a couple of seconds. We overlook the rigorous discipline and dedication of long years that has gone behind an athlete's success. It is easy to walk ten kilometres a day, but it is difficult to walk even one kilometre regularly throughout the year. Here lies the importance of discipline.

80

Choice of Questions

Choosing the questions to answer when there are options in an examination is an art. Only by constant practice can one master this art. A student must not start his exam paper with a mathematical problem. If he commits a mistake right at the start, he needs to scratch it and it makes a bad first impression on the examiner. A student should always start with a comparatively easy question and it must be a theory-type question. In any examination the examiner notices your style of presentation. It is important to start answering in a logical way. Generally, students start writing immediately after getting the question paper. They don't even read the whole question thoroughly. This is not the correct way. Give at least five minutes' time for reading the whole question paper. Be cool. In an exam your mindset plays a great role. Always remember 'Haste is Waste.'

Choosing the right questions has a tremendous impact on the marks you get. If you choose short notes, you must draw the required figures and formulae (if it is a technical subject) instead of writing long notes. You must maintain the proper sequence while answering the questions.

If two students have done the same level of preparation, the one who knows how to choose the questions will excel.

81

No Options Please

While studying any subject always complete the whole syllabus. Nowadays there is a trend to do selective study. In earlier days there were fewer diversions. Nowadays there are diversions from all the corners. Net addiction itself is sufficient to damage a career. Boys and girls don't read the initial chapters of the subjects seriously. Without understanding the basics of the initial chapters they go ahead. To keep pace with other friends and to complete the syllabus they read very fast and literally mug it up. Due to partial understanding, they fail to understand the hard chapters and leave them as optional. At the most they complete 60% to 70% syllabus and based on that half-hearted preparation they go to the exams and certainly fare badly. So one must not go for optional study.

82

How to Adjust with Hostel-mates and Roommates

Many students have to stay in a hostel during the span of their education. In most of the hostels one has to share his room with more than one person. Environment of the hostel plays a major role in a student's mind. Whenever one stays in a hostel, one must have a healthy relationship with his roommates and other inmates of the hostel. If he can't adjust with the hostel atmosphere, he will be cornered, and it will invite complications. Adjustment doesn't mean excessive mixing with one's friends. It means mingling with everybody, but keeping some distance. Adjustment is the key word for being successful in public life. Wherever you stay, if you possess positive thought and helping nature, everybody will like you. Never leave positive thoughts. Food nourishes the body and positive thoughts nourish the soul. From my own experience I do agree that sometimes one may face difficulties in hostel life. In hostel you have to adjust with various kinds of human beings. While living in the hostel you should neither be selfless nor selfish. If you become selfish, friends will abandon you, and you will be confined to your own company. In that case your mental growth will stop. On the other hand, if you become selfless, your friends will exploit you, squeeze you and throw you after use. So you have to be practical. When I shifted to hostel from home after admission to the engineering course, one of my brother's friends told me, 'Enjoy with everybody, but don't allow others to use your room as a common room.' Sometimes it becomes difficult to adapt to the curves of life, but then you can't stop. You may have to judiciously apply the brake of your mind. If you can adjust with your hostel-mates, you can acquire managerial qualities right from your student life without learning management. There are many famous managers who haven't had any formal training in management. Management is basically proper and timely application of your common sense. An experience of hostel life for a couple of years is required for the proper mental growth of every person.

83

A Timetable for Study

Long hours of study without focus or organization doesn't really help. There are students who spend a long time studying, but there won't be anything extraordinary about their results. This is because their method is wrong. Systematic study is essential for success. Hard work and consistency are key to success in an examination. A busy man may get eroded by work pressure, and a lazy man gets corroded by lethargy. Though both are bad, erosion is preferred to corrosion. If you want some work done, give it to a busy man and never to a lazy man. There can be two schedules of study: one for the examination time and the other for the rest of the term. I have given below a sample study timetable for examination time. It can be followed during the preparation leave.

Timetable

7.00–8.00	Morning chores
8.00–11.00	Study
11.00–11.30	Tea-break
11.30–1.00	Study
1.00–2.00	Lunch-break
2.00–5.00	Study
5.00–6.00	Tea-break
6.00–9.00	Study
9.00–10.00	Dinner
10.00–11.30	Study
11.30–7.00	Sleep

Nothing will prevent a student from succeeding if he rigorously follows a timetable of the above kind. You may study for twelve hours one day. But you find it hard to give six hours every day for a fortnight. Consistency and adherence to routine are important but difficult too. Once you try to follow a timetable, you will know how hard it is. But you will also soon realize how effective it is.

84

Be Aware of the Subject Don't Beware of It

Are you frightened by the boards some people display at their gates: 'Beware of Dogs'? Some students are frightened in the same way by their subjects. Also some teachers and seniors intensify it by making a spectre of difficult subjects. They inject fear in the minds of students by projecting certain subjects as hard. At the most they may pass, with a poor score. A comparatively hard subject is to be tackled with the right attitude. Even if you find a subject unnerving, try to enter it and understand it. Continuous effort will make it easy for you.

You should train your mind to face challenges and difficult circumstances. Always remember that however hard an examination may be, there is a section of students who pass it in the very first attempt and with good marks. They have no magical power. Their plus points are hard work, proper method and a clear understanding of the subjects.

Have a fearless mind that will accept the subject as a reality and then face it. Accepting the problem and the readiness to deal with it mean solving half of the problem.

85

Importance of Good Results

'Quality is never an accident, it is always the resultant of an intelligent effort.'

— John Ruskin

To survive in a highly competitive environment, you must have good examination results. Ideally, you should score high in all papers. Here the term 'good result' is used in a relative sense. The minimum requirement is a first class. If you can score enough to win a distinction, it is definitely praiseworthy.

Gaining knowledge is no doubt more important than scoring high. The knowledge will always stand us in good stead. But the world wants to see proof on paper. And in competition an impressive mark sheet counts. It is never just to measure knowledge by the examination score. Nevertheless your score will be what decides your career. If your record isn't good, nobody will ever pay serious attention to you. Therefore, a good result is your trump card for an interview or any other selection procedure.

There are many postgraduates who do not know the basics of their subject, and if asked, they admit as much. We mug up the lesson, commit the text to memory and vomit it out in the examination. We decorate our egos with the degrees we have earned and rest on them for ever. A man with a doctorate will think of a postgraduate as an inferior. The postgraduate in his turn will look down upon a graduate. A degree must not be a means to outsmart others and bolster one's false pride.

86

Your General Knowledge

Every school student must have a good amount of general knowledge. They must know the major events that happen in the world as well as those that happened in the past. Buy a good book of general knowledge. But this is not enough. To keep your general knowledge up-to-date, you must read a standard newspaper every day. Find out what is new in politics, science and sports. Every moment some new information comes in. Give yourself some grounding in general knowledge and keep updating it.

87

Examination Fever

The reason for examination fever is not only the phobia for the examination. In most of the houses the child becomes the victim of comparison. I was always compared with my elder brother, and it irritated me throughout my childhood. This comparison makes students scared of the examination. Comparison injects a pessimistic attitude and nervousness within a child's mind. Psychiatrists can help a child to overcome it, but the guardians' psyche also needs to be changed simultaneously in order to help the child.

One should never think of passing alone. But one must have a higher aim. What can be the worst possible outcome of an examination? One may fail. It must be taken in one's stride. Failure in the examination can be pardoned, but if the mental equilibrium itself is disturbed, that becomes dangerous. One should learn to relax before the examination. Examination is a battle of nerves and that is the reason why one needs to be relaxed. One must not get himself drenched in the drizzle of criticism, but have an umbrella of willpower and confidence to keep it away.

88

How to Overcome Shyness

Some students are excessively shy, and they pay for this nature. In the outer world shyness doesn't pay. A student with a shy nature must come out of his shell and many times this student requires thorough counselling. Sometimes it is better to seek the help of a psychiatrist. That age is very vulnerable. A student goes through a transition, which joins boyhood and manhood. A student's mind contains both the simplicity of a boy and complexity of a man. Many times I have found teachers, especially school-teachers, criticizing a boy with a shy nature. That is absolutely wrong. There are many students who have many doubts, but they never ask a single question in the class because of their shy nature.

> 'To ask a question may bring a moment's shame, but not to ask and remain ignorant is a life-time of shame.'
>
> — Anonymous

A shy student must try to overcome his shyness, otherwise he is bound to suffer in this smart world. They should try again and again and till the end they must continue their effort. Here is another piece of wisdom.

> 'Being defeated is often a temporary condition, giving up is what makes it permanent.'
>
> — Marilyn vos Savant

How true it is! You must have heard the story of Robert Bruce, who was inspired by a spider. One must not surrender. Another name of surrender is death of mind. There is no substitute to willpower. Tremendous amounts of talent and energy are present in each human being. Nobody will help you. It is you who has to awaken himself. During the crucifixion, Jesus Christ carried his own cross. If Lord Jesus could help himself, why not we?

89

Importance of Teamwork

Teamwork has tremendous power.A team with good tuning can multiply the efficiency of a person by many times, and the total output can be unimaginable. We Indians lack in teamwork. In a team everyone must be without ego, and no one should count his contribution. One shouldn't take the stress alone. Big ventures are not possible without a good team. If there is defeat, share it; it will reduce. If there is joy, share it too. It will multiply. Whether it is the design of a bridge, a one-day cricket match or an open-heart surgery, the success or failure depends on the team. In a team the role of the team leader or captain is very important. Life is just like an echo. If the leader motivates his member and doesn't keep any distance from his team members, they can do miracles. On the other hand, because of his ego, if the leader or captain separates himself from the rest of the team, the team is bound to fail. So whenever you have to go with others, you must show good sportsmanship. If you wish, you can achieve so much. The success is not beyond your reach.

90

Your School Magazine

Be a part of your school magazine team, either by writing for the magazine or by being a member of the magazine committee. You may write factual articles, poems, stories or anything of your choice. Some good school magazines include interviews with famous people. The school elects the students who will interview these people. Try to be one among the interviewers. But unless you are good at studies and smart, the school will not include you in the team. So be studious and smart.

Contribute your suggestion for the cover of the magazine, layout, colours and overall appearance.

91

How to Score More in the Examination

How to score more in the examination is an important question. We often hear students say that in spite of giving a good exam they get low marks and the result is below their expectations. In ninety-nine per cent of cases we see the same thing. If the answer sheets are shown to the students, they will realize which are the places where they have committed mistakes. Generally, there are two major reasons why the students secure low marks. First is inadequate practice, and the second is lack of counselling. These are a few points that need to be followed for securing good marks in exams:

i) Know the basics of every subject.
ii) Complete the syllabus.
iii) Attend all the classes and try to avoid taking leave.
iv) Study every subject for at least half an hour every day.
v) Get proper counselling from your guardians and friends.

vi) Don't study just for the marks. If you study well, marks will come automatically.

vii) Give special efforts for those subjects in which you are weak or the subjects you don't like.

viii) Take dummy tests to get the feel of an exam.

ix) Learn time management.

x) Be careful about unit conversions when a problem contains different unit systems.

xi) Never use red pen or pencil; leave margins in your answer sheet properly.

xii) Write your roll number on the main answer booklet as well as on the supplementary answer sheets and tie them properly.

xiii) Don't forget to cancel the rough work done by you by criss-cross lines at the end of the exam.

xiv) Number the pages. If there are sixteen pages then number them like 1/16, 2/16, 3/16 ... 16/16.

xv) Check all the sums immediately after solving them.

xvi) Read the questions properly and be judicious while selecting them.

xvii) Start your exam with a comparatively easy theoretical question, so that there will not be any mistake at the start.

xviii) Try to have a good handwriting. If it is not very good at least it must be legible.

xix) Answer questions in a sequential manner. Suppose there are question numbers 1a, 1b, 1c, 2a, 2b and

2c. A candidate may answer them in the following sequence: 2c, 1a, 1c, 2b, 1b and 2a. No one can object, but if the candidate follows the pattern 1a, 1b, 1c, 2a, 2b and 2c then it will be more impressive.

xx) Take weekly practice tests and get your papers checked by your teacher, home tutor or parents. Then easily you will be able to locate which are the mistakes generally committed by you.

If a school kid follows these twenty points he can score more in any exam.

92

First Week after Vacation

Most of the students become lethargic when the school reopens after vacation. Initially they can't concentrate on their studies. Their big mistake is that during vacation the students don't touch the books. During exams they study for 8–10 hours a day but during vacation they don't even study for half an hour. Please keep this important suggestion in your mind. During the time of examinations through rigorous studies, you attain a good level and just after the exam when the vacation starts, you totally stop your practice. Due to that again your level comes down. After vacation when you start the preparation again you need to reach the previous level and it takes long time to attain it. But if you just keep on practising (at least for half an hour per day) you can retain your level and you won't lose anything. So, don't be lethargic after vacations and work hard.

93

Informal Get-together

An informal get-together of school students makes a great difference. We go to school every day, but this is quite a routine and formal affair. An informal get-together helps us discover one another.

In a school the students of class ten arranged a get-together. Each student was to perform something. The children put up a show of their creative talents. There was a shy girl who generally remained silent in the class and who was not good in studies. When her turn came, this girl sang beautiful *ghazals*, which amazed everybody. Nobody thought she was so talented. This is one example of how an informal get-together can bring out the hidden talents in us. This proves that only with academics, other activities also must receive importance in our school life.

94

Don't Neglect Maths!

Many students are afraid of mathematics. It is really a prejudice. Those who instil this prejudice in children's mind include parents, friends, teachers and neighbours. The fear of mathematics has nothing to do with the subject, but the conditioning.

Mathematics is not a subject like history. One can understand modern history without reading ancient history. But without understanding trigonometry one can't learn calculus.

People have always thought mathematics a difficult subject. The way parents, teachers and classmates talk about mathematics also bias children against the subject. If you tell a good student, 'Beware of maths. It's difficult and you'll suffer miserably', he is bound to perform badly because of a defeated morale, even if he is a good student. But if the same student is told, 'Go ahead, you are really fast with maths! You will beat everyone in maths!', he is sure to do well in the exam.

A subject like mathematics cannot be mastered overnight. It requires slow and continuous practice. So start building your strong foundation in mathematics, which will ensure your success in the future.

95

Use Your Failure for Future Success

Often we take the failures of our life seriously. But from each failure we can learn many things. Once a boy prepared for a subject at the eleventh hour and appeared for the examination. Obviously, he failed in the exam. He was depressed and was sorry that he failed only by two marks. He filled the form for retotalling and revaluation. After retotalling and revaluation, his marks didn't change. The boy also knew very well that he didn't deserve the pass marks. Then he started preparing for the subject sincerely and gradually developed interest in the subject. In the first attempt he had prepared half-heartedly and he didn't have any love or respect for the subject and he just wanted to get rid of it. If he had passed that time it would be just like getting a lottery and surely he would have thrown the books into the bin after passing.

But the second time, when he started studying seriously, he developed interest in the subject and gradually started loving the subject. The subject was physical chemistry and the course was B.Sc. Then he decided to study further in the same line and wanted to pursue chemical engineering after completing B.Sc. He did that. After completion of his graduation in chemical engineering he completed M.Tech in rubber technology, and today he is the CEO of a company that is famous for producing tyres of international standard. This is the picture of life. From this we can conclude that even failures can change your life in the positive direction provided you accept them with the right frame of mind.

96

Just Do Your Work; Result Will Come Automatically

A mistake we commit very often is that we plan too much for our future. I find boys and girls thinking of placements right from the first year of their graduation. This is the time to study. If you perform well, the result is bound to be good. If you care and nurture a sapling, within a few days it will grow, and after certain months it will bloom with flowers. On the contrary, if you just dream up a tree full of flowers without even planting one, it will just remain a dream.

Once in a school there were two friends. Both of them decided to choose medicine as there future line of study. One of them commented, 'After becoming a doctor I would charge at least hundred rupees per patient.' This incident took place in 1982. The hundred rupees in 1982 is equivalent to at least Rs300 today. Just think of the price of petrol in 1982. The other boy didn't comment. After five years both of them completed their graduation in medicine and started practising. The first candidate failed miserably in his medical practice. He was only interested in money. He decided to take at least one hundred rupees fees per patient but hardly was there any patient who came to him for consultation. On the contrary, the second boy was not money-minded. His fee was only Rs20 and for the poor people he used to give free consultation and for the very needy he used to give free samples of medicines given to him by medical representatives. His clinic used to be crowded with patients. He was a good doctor and through continuous practice his knowledge increased to a great extent. The more cases a doctor does, the wider will be his range of knowledge. So the conclusion is: just do your work, the result will come automatically.

97

Be Decent

However intelligent a student may be unless he or she is decent it is of no use. The root cause of most of the problems is pride. Please note one thing: in every class there is only one topper but dozens of backbenchers. If the topper throws his weight around and becomes boastful, nobody will care for him. The world doesn't care for your first rank or gold medal. People in general only value good behaviour.

In a school in Pune both the first- and second-rank-holders were girls. The girl who used to get the second rank was very proud and she always used to distance herself from others which made her unpopular among her friends. Truly speaking, she didn't have any friends. Only one or two girls of the same nature used to accompany her. They were highly negative at core. She didn't even have respect for the teachers. What did she achieve except the second position? She earned only the curse of the teaching community and hatred of her classmates. She was pugnacious. Even for half a mark she used to argue with the teachers in an indecent manner. She always tried her best to increase some marks in the unit tests through the art of negotiation because in the unit tests teachers return the answer sheets to the students.

On the other hand the first-rank-holder was decent, polite and down-to-earth. She knew very well that the world doesn't care for her first rank. She used to help everybody. She used to give her notes even to the back-benchers for copying. Quite often the backbenchers used to be absent and afterwards no one was ready to lend them the notes. She used to give her notes to them and they used to copy them. She knew that knowledge would increase if you distribute it.

We have a typical tendency. We want to keep even the cheapest thing under lock and key. Why is it so? By giving to others you won't become poor. The first-rank-holder was immensely popular among students. Education and academics helped her a lot. But the thing that helped her the most was her decent and down-to-earth nature.

98

Be Your Own Teacher

In this world you can be your best teacher. But how do you teach yourself? Can a person teach himself? Yes, he can! There is a special way of doing that. Introspect. Ask yourself what your strong and weak points are. Then jot down those points and write down your goals. Regularly ask yourself how much you have improved. You are bound to improve if you keep a consistent record of your weak points and strong points.

A small boy in a village school was a slow writer. He could solve at the most four sums in an hour. His parents didn't have any hope because always the boy used to attempt only a part of any question paper in the examination. Hardly ever did he attempt 60 per cent of the total questions. Though he knew everything, because of his slow pace of writing he was incapable of completing the paper.

Then the parents brought him to a career counsellor in the nearby city and the counsellor counselled the child for one hour. He asked the child to watch him solving the problems and observe the time required to solve each of the problems. The child started practising it and today after one year of regular and rigorous practice he is able to solve ten problems per hour. That means his efficiency increased considerably. This is a clear example of how one can motivate himself and how one can be one's own best teacher.

99

You Can Succeed

You can succeed provided you follow the rules for achieving success. It is easier to attain success than retain it. Follow these rules of success:

i) Have a positive aim.
ii) Never have low self-esteem.
iii) Don't be influenced by others.
iv) Try to lean the core of a subject, never be happy with superficial knowledge.
v) Don't be proud, have team spirit and be logical and rational.
vi) Never be shaky while asking doubts.
vii) Don't copy others. Have your own style and try to have your own brand name.
viii) Help others. You won't get money by helping others but their blessings and good wishes will be there with you for the future.
ix) Never compromise with your own choice in the stream of study.

x) Don't adopt a particular branch of study just for money. Go for that line which you like. If you go for your preferred branch, you will automatically earn a good amount of money, and if you earn relatively less, even then it won't matter much because you will have the convictions for pursuing the preferred subject.

xi) Be straightforward, but don't hurt others.

xii) Work less but work regularly.

xiii) Have love for your profession, colleagues and others who come into close contact with you.

xiv) Don't sleep during daytime.

xv) Have control over watching television.

xvi) Don't see too many matches on the TV, better you play some matches.

xvii) Practice, practice and practice! There is no substitute to it.

xviii) Take practice tests and get your exam papers corrected by your teachers.

xix) Have respect for your parents and be loving, caring and sharing.

xx) Have optimized ambition, it will be easy to reach that step by step.

100

You Will Definitely Succeed

There is hundred per cent guarantee that you will succeed provided you put in the required efforts and practise regularly. There is nothing called 'impossible'. Impossible is a word that exists in the dictionary of cowards. Once there was a boy who had polio. He was partially crippled. But later by the dint of hard work, punctuality, perseverance and planning he became a medal winner in the Olympics. If a polio patient can win the Olympic medal, can't you get through an examination? Yes, you must be motivated.

Have you ever seen an artificial limb centre? I have. People who have lost both their hands perform many of the regular activities just using their legs. I saw a teenager draw beautiful sketches with his leg because he had lost his hands. Is it easy? Not at all. It is really difficult but in front of strong willpower even the most difficult task of the world bows down. Have a strong willpower, delete the word 'impossible' from the dictionary of your mind and go ahead with the speed of lightning. The sunrise of tomorrow is exclusively reserved for you and there is success in store for you. It is nothing but the result of your intelligent planning and hard work coupled with the benediction of the Almighty. Even sky is not the limit. I am sure, that day is not very far when you will engrave your name in the academic landscape of this universe with golden letters. Follow these four lines throughout your life.

> 'Good, better, best
> Do not rest
> Till good be better
> And better best.'

Notes

Notes

Notes

Notes

Notes